to my favorite painter & hero
—emilio villalba

WORD CAVE

To. Alex Kanevsky & Hollis Heichemer,
How lovely to know you both.
Hope you find some verse
to enjoy in here.

love & respect,

26 oct 2020

WORD CAVE

Tamsin Spencer Smith

RiskPress

Published by RiskPress Foundation
825 Gravenstein Highway North, Suite 12
Sebastopol, California 95472
pkcp@aol.om

All rights reserved.

Published in the United States of America
Copyright © Tamsin Spencer Smith, 2018

ISBN 978-0-9848403-5-9

Cover painting by Emilio Villalba
www.emiliovillalbaart.com

Inside cover flap photographs by Josh Smith
www.joshsmithphoto.com

Inside cover photograph by Una Ryan
www.uluxart.com

Back cover collage by Matt Gonzalez
www.dolbychadwickgallery.com/artists/matt-gonzalez

Book design by Charlie Pendergast and Kevin Connor
RiskPress Foundation: pkcp@aol.com

Printed in China by Global PSD
Special thanks to Adrianne and Anne

For Matt

Acknowledgments

A good bit of the practice of poetry stems from a desire to see and be seen, to touch and be touched — by the world at large, but even more importantly, by the people in it. It can be a lonely pursuit. I am thus eternally grateful for the following individuals who have made it feel much less so. They have each listened, urged, and shaped me and my verse for the better. Matt Gonzalez, Charlie Pendergast, Kevin Connor, Lisa Chadwick, Dana Gioia, Peter Reiling, Ben Dunlap, Mary Julia Klimenko, Mark degli Antoni, Ana Teresa Fernandez, Christine Olsen, Ali Fenn, Rachael Lamkin, Christine Mason, my mother Una Ryan, my sister Amy Dowsett, and my children Scully and Tabitha. Muses all.

Contents

Author's Note

The purpose of Paleolithic cave paintings remains a mystery. Were they a way for prehistoric people to communicate essential information? Did they capture ceremonial or religious devotions? Or, were they simply the imaginative musings of an early artist?

We may never know the answers to these questions. That may be the best part. Veiled messages from the distant past remain a source of ongoing wonder. Their beauty feels raw and thrilling, and moves us in ways we can't quite define. They speak to some primal part of us that is deeper than knowing.

To me, this is the state of wonderment that poetry invites us to enter. It's a realm of intimate secrets, in which we are enticed to become more fully alive. There is a mysticism to this process that requires poetry to transcend even its own building blocks. Language itself learns to shapeshift in order to sneak past the mind's defenses. When we by-pass the logic circuit that seeks certainty, we gain awareness of fresh ways to experience the inner and outer world.

How a poem is crafted is central to widening, deepening, and extending the sensations of possibility that it prompts. When I write verse, I usually begin with a particular memory or emotion that is itching to get out. Yet the task of proceeding is never direct. If I simply pinned words to the page, the life might seep out of the poem. My goal is to make each poetic word cave pulse with dynamic energy.

To effect this transmutation, I experiment with different styles, forms, and techniques. I take care in selecting words and phrases that have power to refract in divergent directions. Unique or surprising images are designed to invite you to step inside the story. Meter or rhyme appear in hopes of making you sway a little. The verse becomes a word cave when it is your shadows that begin to flicker and dance upon the walls.

Know too that when you move down the corridors of a poem, line breaks can be read as corners to turn or places to rest. These are questions to embrace. Try reading the line as a continuation or a full stop. What you take away may change. Ideally, the poems will keep stirring and unfolding over time. Their layers are yours now. They belong to you.

On a final note, the title of this collection is inspired the Romanian-born poet Paul Celan, who wrote in German, even though he associated his mother tongue with those who had killed his family and so many others in the 1940s. In treating words themselves as beings in need of resurrection and perhaps redemption, he created gorgeous, unique verse that breathes with palpable intensity. Pierre Joris' English translations are especially poignant, particularly "Line the Wordcaves", which remains a touchstone.

Not To Diminish

Imaginary Landscape

Not the elimination of decisions
This procession by chance
Rather an allowance for different possibilities
An accretion of space

Lines drawn, composed, or played at random
Stand supremely
Unique, unrepeatable
Yet still connected

Their grace and purpose
Move in quiescence
An even open
Eternal – maybe

Erasure too is a form of unfolding
Like the resolution of a mystery
A revelation relaxing
Stricture structure

Try to treasure the ephemeral
The way frame by frame
The whitening of a canvas
Eliminates all borders

The moral of this story
That it must be told
To know
We no longer need it

[Composer John Cage devoted his music to the exploration of non-intention. He used the chance operations of the I Ching to select what notes to play, removing from the mix, choice, ego, taste, and even the desire to please. He lived the questions. This is hard to do in art, in life.]

Variations in a Minor Key

I

In my experience
The most tangible refrains
Are the broken ones

You and I
We gather up
Our pieces

Things dropped
Or knocked over
Long ago

Shards press together
Palm to bloody palm
A syntax of ache

As our mouths
Exchange a solemn secret
Sealing an irretrievable gift

However we arrived here
Whatever we are doing
On our knees

In this moment
Pleading
Is forever ours

I know that I will
Never understand this
And I know that this

Not knowing
Denies nothing
That not knowing holds

A truth
Like a poem
Like a love

Audible
Only beyond
The lines

II

Compass, thermometer, time bomb, slave
Why of all the earth's loveliness
Are we so ruled?

The human heart
Each a secret dog whistle
Black box record of flight

Perhaps we paint our poems to charm
The devils inside
As if they could

Behave, requite

True Story

for Zio Ziegler

Everything contained within the painted detail
Passages, portents, empires of color
Care, time, loin and will, habits of being

Form linked stories, each an island wound with
Moody limbic limbs, complex of wordless
Cries, infinite mouth pitch of lamp or mars black

As the burnt wood shade of cave figures
Press though the idea of you to what is
You the penumbra, eclipse of the self

Perfect shadow boundary alight so fringe
Becomes focus becomes its own
True story

[Artists will refine a certain style only then to obliterate what makes it most
identifiable. It takes courage to step outside of the tales we take on. In the corner
of my friend Zio Ziegler's studio, I came across a canvas with an identifiably
Zioesque figure over which he had painted a stark outline akin to the tape that
marks a crime scene death. It spoke to an emergence. I followed that thought.]

Present Future

The best presents show their age
The weight of their edges
Like hands ribboning hips
In anticipation of the slow pulling
Open to a memory
One day you'll have
Of tumbling into flight
Whispering things you sense
You already knew
Illuminating interior lights
Invisible to the crowd
Heat shaded stars below the skin
As sea tossed glass
As thrown off wrappings
Salt and dust
The texture of honor well worn
Moored in heart's cove
Artifact of all possible in times
When poets make prophets of the blind
And burnt offerings to rosy-fingered dawn

ITCH

Mutable metronome below the bone
Slow this pulse to the paler pattern of ancient permissions
Cast between the wide net of wish and stumbling
Two fish

One answers to body; the other to mind
Twinned shadows
They form infinite liquid loops
Working the water back upon itself

In tonight's particular dream
I float suspended
Buoyant bridge
Between thought and feeling

Above me
Night's canopy flickers
Ghost light of stars
Long-lingering tales of initial intent

When did saying something
Become an act
Of trying to say something

What gets displaced
As I move through the river
Words folding back upon themselves

Remember a time when hovering hands
Beamish to the quick
Fingertip to fingertip trembling

Beat out something true
Upon this drum
Of skittish verse

Taut and teaching skin
A carnal canvas
Lifting in relief

An atlas
Of longing transitive
Upon your lips

Itch
The noun : a torment
The verb : bliss

Dear,

They believed
The ancient Greeks
That a river called Ocean
Surrounded the world

I believe
This half of To and From
That an ocean like a fever
Can't be outrun

There are no lines
In space
Legends, labels
Self-erase

Maps
Even words
Turn on themselves
Blurring

Thus doldrums
Argue stasis
Denial veers
Over there

But here, *au contrair*

In my equatorial region
Winds rise up

Storm from still water,
Low pressure to squall

There is a physical law to every convergence

When warm air like close breath belts
Calms we can name
Tropic of Cancer, Tropic of Capricorn,
These Horse Latitudes

I am undone
At a vanishing point
Inked
By the slow compression of tears

Into this :

The weather is here
Wish you were

You
Were
Always
Beautiful

Soundings

Departure lounge socket
Juicing my device
Your text arrives
Bring me dirt

To this day, exchanges with you
Leave phrase-tattoos
Staccato etchings beneath the skin
Above the surface of memory

Lifting then dropping
As a wave
Raking
Sand and sundry

Trips away from you
More than a few
That first one
An ancient haunting place

Tropical birds and cobblestones
Soundless volcanoes surround from every direction
And then the next voyage more birds
A deep continent of music missing only yours

And then a long wall
Which wound the full landscape
Visible even to the moon
As a scar

Centuries
Of ancestors
Enjoined
Past regret

Followed
It must be said
By silence
Not listening

I don't know
Really
How it was
That again

Cobblestones
Mist
Hushed hands holding
A lost city in the distance

Secret Chord

I have listened for you in twilight's soft shell of wonder
Reckoned slant soundings
At the crook of lonely dawn
Conjured words and swallowed them
In the same breath

Sacred words
I have felt the touch of you
As a world lush with meadow bloom
Greets a summer sigh's
Glissade to Autumn

I watched as the sky
Fell to the darkness of the lake
And the distant ribbon of a train
Fluttered by
Without a whistle

Questions of Scintillation

How does it feel
Skin soft slipped
From fullest flex
Bare against your back
Breath dwelling
In-prelude out-rendezvous
Self of your sleeping self
Circling all centers
Of sloped certainty
From silver sky coin
To smooth sea surface
Not minding
Which is moon
Which smooth liquid
Sine phase switches
Me on
Every cell a blaze
Can you tell

Impression of a Lone Arc Floating

The open space
Between head and heart
Lies here at Lands End

I hover
Ever
At the edge of things

Watching
This city bob
Like Atlantis in the mist

At ease she beckons
Gathering the hemlines of my hungry mind
Like silk, she sweeps them up the leg of her shore

My thoughts wicking higher to thigh
Torso salt-tasting
Weightless sand

Her sand like skin
Shimmering
Sand-skin shivering sea foam sighs

Surrendering sighs as waves
Tendering
Naked as a sieve gives

Shell shards, half whorls, star shadows,
Driftwood, damp grass, moon scales, charms
Patterns & passages

Each breath-born bubble
A broom of fluid thought
More vast than forgetting

Scooped upon my palm
Blooming

Ode Abridged

Fog veiled I could be a wind-strung harp
Laid down by a languid god
Sole spine cresting a chorus of waves
Tuned by mortal applause

Hear in these notes a wonted reprise
Your melody buckle to mine
Our everest wish: for spirits that soar
Wide-winged with an ache sublime

No fault, nor tremor can break the flight
Of a free form tethered in air
Give a sign, cast a line
An oar, a shore, a dare

Join rock-socket soul to shear-link dream
In union we meet our test
Move through my islands, arise and come
Be transported (Thy East upon My West)

This wandering verse may time traverse
Let first-feelings whisper true
For all we can claim of an anchor in life
Is a sea-sifted *pas de deux*

[This poem was inspired by a construction tour of the new eastern span of the Bay Bridge. The language of engineers is rich with metaphor, as is so much of what surrounds us.]

Silence on the Tongue

Silence slices
Open the mind
Until we taste

Layered loss seasoned
With savory naked need
Hard bitten

Between the textures of timid time and
Sensation : bitter, sweet, sour, salty, and
(Savor its time on the tongue)
umami

Desire densifies
When spread with will

Wedged and bursting
Our lips search out

Hand-torn folds draping
The trim edge of factory-cut forms

A thin pin holds the whole
Aloft as a spine

Until something
Winks at nothing

And we swallow

Oblique Strategies

Trust your body
To make the right mistakes
Roll for higher stakes

In the hay
Trust your lust
Release the stay

One hand can't hold
What two unfold
Embrace Adjust

[Simple aphorisms can help break creative blocks. Musician Brian Eno and Fine
Artist Peter Schmidt collaborated on a deck of "Oblique Strategy" cards, each
of which contains a saying that they have used to prompt lateral thinking. This
poem was written after drawing two such cards.]

Succulent

I treasured that generous spray
Overtopping its terracotta pot
As full of more than I could say
And more softly

A peace offering perhaps
Gestured kindness
Both needing to touch something alive
That rained-out day

These months later
Distance crossed
I can confess to you
Now its loss

An imbalance of water or light
Green shoots shrunk to nought
You said it wasn't a sign
The reader is always right

The Double

Time will come
Your eyes will no longer open
This ill-kempt world
Your hurried life out lapped
By its own ceaseless striving
You'll find yourself in a four-sided forest
Trees signing vernacular shapes
A younger you understood
The air night-vision green
Whirs with the rattle of grass spears
As appears a form perceived as other
You start as though waking
Imagine it has been chasing you
Only to find you are the one who pursues
This union of all your acts and offerings
Over all your years upon this orb
Lie down within yourself
Regain the gift
You made this life
There is no other

Lady Daze

*Aquarius – During this fast paced but rather difficult week,
you`re bound to go through several versions of plans.
That being said, take a chance on something new or unfamiliar
and focus on what you can learn.*

Whispers scorch
Legs blaze
Laughter in reverse
Over and above
The necessary plank
Steps
Meanwhile
One planet sextilles another
A cusp is crossed

Mercury

I seldom get the science square
As hope is to logic; so vapor to air

The weight of a cloud — what a terrible scare
That's like, 200 pachyderms, per cumulus pair

But, boiling point, gravity, conversion and scale
Precepts of nature, quests for the grail

These hide a truth beyond chartings of old
A slow-found element more precious than gold

This compound is formed through base human pleasure
Such tactile delight trumps chemical measure

Its properties are simply thus
Without need of rhyme : us
Or worry that the toxicity of vermillion may muddle my metaphor : us

You are weather
To my ocean

Moving with the moon (still)
Rising in sun (not still)

Quick-silver

Entirely
Up

Leviathan

Call me *Ish* he says
Not one for quick introductions
I grow nervous with the familiar

Take what you must of this world he says
Mine the flat land, drain the swirling ocean, hunt as the hunted

A long white stone turns all centers
A plinth in an antique sea
Behind curtains of seaweed and sail, beasts crouch in wait

The narrator's voice booms
Dislodging the stars he so meticulously placed
Every choice is a cipher
Stop playing the haunted parts

Flash bulbs of lost consciousness
Capture the folly of the scene
Bodies of thought scatter
Startled there must be
Something to our hero's journey
The vast grey seems to stretch only so far

Like Honey

We search for life amongst the perishable things
And where better but a landscape of littered longing
For arrival, for return, something familiar, something rare
Do we ever really care what we seek beyond the yen
Or is homecoming the self-same act evading despair

The way we seduce our own memories
The way we coax to regret again
One more fleeting kiss
As if amber —

Suspended sap, healing glow, fossilized tear —

Flowed
Sweet and slow
Like honey

Step

for Ana Teresa Fernandez

She pours herself in
Slippers of glass
Princess of modern
Mistress of cool water

Tight fit
Cast perfect
Frozen ankle turning
Body fever burning

Surface shifting
Side to side
Melting myth
Platforms subside

Bare at last
Skin to ground
Goddess her
Own self unbound

[Artist ATF created ice stilettos and stood in them as they melted over a subway grate to reframe a classic fairy tale.]

Renoir's Queen

for Ana Teresa Fernandez

She is not one
She is only one
She is the only one
She is all color
Or the absence of

She conveys
Without you
Or needing you to hear
Stay
Fear

Feather-banded ankles
Sweep the night sky
Sins of stars effaced
Their camouflage erased
By cutting eights
Upon a flour brushed floor

White teeth shout silence
Innocence
Outlines are orchestrated
To foreground
Exposures multiplied

Compensation for another
Intensity
Oil of walnut
Soot of coal
Resin of pine

Distill us
Darkling prism
Mend the broken root
Paint pure
Shade

Huellas
Sombras
Lagrimas
Negras
Nos

[Artist ATF "erased" her body by painting it black in solidarity with the 43 young male students from Ayotzinapa, Mexico still missing and presumed to have been disappeared for their political protest. Auguste Renoir once claimed black was the "queen of all colors"]

Gauntlet

worn

run   through

thrown   down

taut

              t a u n t

g a u n t

        l e t

n a u g t

        g e t

you confront what?

                      when confronted

These Ithakas

They mistook the busyness of her hands
The doing and undoing as nothing
But nerves — more the mastery

Her mixing with tapered fingers
Light against loom
Helms of hope and vatic beam

Now until then winding warp and web
Time's fabric fretted by curses and crossing
Briny islands, bleaching sun, a winnowing fan, and further

Lunar blush, in mist and all
Her hands shape a beggars bowl
A tempered sword, candor of siren, shape-shifting caress

On canvas, the forging of a shield
And as ever, waves wish their way
Up cliffs out-running cunning caves

And again rivers rise
Memory grey-eyed willing
In fog, a motion — there

Stretch out a thread
Another day
Drawn beyond the dawn

Another day
Weaving home

Feels Like You

a poet
would find a way
press your hips into wax
push your hands through water
                              stroking

dig   dig
rise when it comes
              voice in your ear
two extra paddles
          to match
vertebrae   a whole column bow
          braced at the surge space
                    wave spout shock-thrusts
                          hesitation
                                back down your throat
                                    legs swing round

                  you and you
                              are now so totally
                                                    up

                        on it
slide-switched
        every cell *on*
                like you finally get   it
                              all
                          of   it
long-ridden
          walking on water
                      cipher-breaking   cry of the gull
                                          his   your own
voice
          praying
                    waving
                            wanting
courage to say
                    nothing in the world…

Vacancy

Smoke-choked corridors
Ash in trays spilling
Centuries of blackened books
Smote, their splendid stories
Survived by stubborn spines
      Numb to the specter of cracking
It's all boneyard now

But for one soul
Plunking keys
No one registers anymore
Not rooms   not chords
Schubert, Basie, Monk
Struck dumb
      Be voiceless guest
Dead languages clog pipes
At the Motel Ambos Mundos

Flora
Fauna
The least of what's lost
It wasn't even bombs exploding —
Packs on the backs of children exploding —
Temples   theaters   parks exploding —
It was the empty stares
Stare upon stare in the streets of cities
Screen-blank masks shuffling
Past piles and piles of shoes
On beaches baking

Shoe upon shoe
Each staring
With torn tongue

Lone neon cry

The only sign of life
At the Ambos Mundos

Imago

for Tabitha Spencer on her 12th birthday

Early arriver
Assured Aquarian
Full forged command soft sovereign
Rule each due and day as your own
Stride self serene
Unfolding bright dominion
Dragonfly wise
Iridescent on the wing
Nimble, strong, clear
Sage, the way Plato meant it
My shy teacher

What can I beyond you impart?

Sorrow and some loss
Cannot be strangers to a rich heart
Connector that you are
Bind steel to sensibility
Convey cognition
With level eyes gaze on fair form
Stoke inner stilled glow
Beneath bone
Beguiling smile
Trust true action
Cohere to kind

Don't spin sails searching
Be a maker
Forge
Friendship

Beauty
Tolerance
Banish boredom
The impossible
The conventional

Open what's stuck
Even from within
Repatriate possibility
Pardon the brave

Surrender only to thine own
Velvet paw
Be good
Stay gentle

Always know
I love you +
Grammar matters
Except in poems

[The word *imago* signifies the mature stage of a winged insect and the unconscious sense of a person, commonly a parent, who guides behavior.]

Janus

Gateway god
Face of beginnings
Peace and war
What happens next
What came before

No rhyme elides
The other side
Blind spots
Questions we never bothered to ask
Do you remember that time amongst the ruins?
Tourists made myopic by their long-lensed garlands
The guide's supreme patience
Or was it boredom

In another time
That rubble might have been a corridor
Some more direct route to safety
But by then it was hard to recognize anything
For what it had been, might be
And us?
Walls, passages, stone remains

Fractals

Augury : jockey and horse eye to eye; a sun's unseen march down concrete, omen from the west

Urn : what are you doing with your life?

Want : chrysalis form of courage

Fur : kindness, consistently, when no one is looking

Despite : seconds and days, waiting and watching

Rust : problems of translation, a robin's call, have a nice life in texted hieroglyphics

Drift : arrested development, conventional wisdom, what they say (see Urn)

Containment : mental marching

Veil : for all the lines on sea and sky, Homer never mentions blue, the color of no natural flower

Moon : as in silver apples of, as in dance, as in river, as in every still pond, stolen wishes

Audacity : a plant that is not violets, confusion of indigo, lazy boat floating

Gingery : connecting without and within, a sleight of hand

Clay : a rift, the major key, judicious exercise

Minor chord : moth wing, window, wide-eyed, the search for proof

Paint : a building up, effort, both the opposite and apotheosis of effacement

Sculpt : to reveal, to be revealed

Golondrina

Amor asciende en una nota clara
Pero un corazón se rompe en sinfonía

En los movimientos mayor y menor
Los recuerdos se estrellan
Olas de bronce, cuerda, tripa

Espíritu del ser
Es fantasma de cada melodía
La forma en que un arco dibuja el dolor

Libera vibraciónes
Que enlaza el principio y su fin

En un instante
Por un vuelo de manos

Swallow

Love ascends in one clear note
But a heart breaks in symphony
In movements major and minor
Memories crash
Waves of brass, string, gut
Spirit of self
Haunts each melody
The way a bow draws pain
Releases vibration
Binds beginning and end
In an instant
By the flight of hands

[Written for new friends in Sayulita, Mexico]

Carousello or Little War

Riding round and round
Used to feel merry
I knew so well the rise and fall
Of the green mare in front
Blue to my left
Black-maned bay on the right
Self-same revolve
Painted tail, gilded part
Some of us fixed to the slip-safe platform
Others bobbing the brassy poles
Who chose? Makers, I suppose

I should try
At least peer past
The romance side
Beyond the rounding boards
I've never looked anyone not even myself
In the eye
In candor
Everyone wears blinders
Revolves around their own alternating reflection
Pointing at flashes
Familiar, fanciful, afeared

Children especially
In shock or reckless glee
Stalk interior mirrors
Ignoring crowd shouts
Hunting their own faces

As masks among menagerie
My rider
Boy of ten
Sees what looking back from the glass?
I don't know
He whispers low
we must go
we must go
Arms about my neck
Heels hammer hard
Battering blows at my wooden side

I gallop faster
here we go
Flank freed from itself
Ring of splinters rain
A clockwise gyre

Then a great hush
Whirlitzer silenced
People cover eyes, mouths
As I'm lifted
Freed from these bolts
Set beside a booth
Madame Zita stirs
Fan of cards, wavering wand
Nodding crystal clarity
She selects a fate to drop
From the slot
The boy now at my side
Bends to read :

Opportunities multiply as they are seized

[The word "carousel" comes from *carosello* (Italian). Its roots lie in a medieval jousting ritual used to prep Knights for combat. Horsemen refined their skills by riding in tight circles, tossing balls back and forth. Such "little war" games stretch even farther back to Byzantine and Arab traditions, before re-emerging in Europe during the Crusades. The closing aphorism comes from Sun Tzu's *The Art of War.*]

Another Poet Dials the Sun

What's it like to act
Never less than
You are independent
Of audience
Outside forecast
Historic high or low

Perfectly at home
In solitary dominion
Or drifting in and out
Hazy stratus negligees, mare's tails, mackerel skies
Ever clear on what to wear
Is it disco balls all the way down?

Totally sunny semblance
Even when the world is not
That's what got Frank O'Hara
To look up more often
How you double-barreled Mayakovsky
Teamed up like twin lights to elude prison grey

You don't have to visit me
Too minor to be poet #3
A simple sign will show
The "they" who made you go
Still call
So one day
I might

[Shyly, I step into the shadow of Vladimir Mayakovsky's "An Extraordinary
Adventure Which Happened to Me in a Summer Cottage" and Frank O'Hara's
response "A True Account of Talking to the Sun at Fire Island".]

Full Fathom Five

for Una S. Ryan

Satellite spy hole
Lay over alleged differences
Wed atoll to atmosphere
Align these anatomies crosswise
Cellular sub-self and topographic supra-self
Crux-limbed like lovers
Lost ligature coupled

Supplicant fugitives
We stand at the threshold
Our magnified inner arbors
Panning coins for human tolls
Searching safe passage in the subtlest fugue
You a branch — I a stream
Bridges bear no allegiance to side

        For eye muscle mimics the careful twist
        Of Jackson Pollock's *Lavender Mist*
        Balances of ear is born upon
        Sea-change bell of Ariel's song
                & *Diabelli Variations*
                          of Ludwig van

Tympanic triggers
Call castaways on cue
Coral kingdom rise
From meteor and mandible
Not one island
Ever beyond rescue

[My mother turns science into art by fusing satellite images of the earth from space with electron micrographs of freeze-fractured blood and lung cells. The images capture in exquisite detail the intense beauty of all that unites us inside and far beyond. The result is a sort of sacred geometry that the body recognizes before the mind does. Other examples of this fractal phenomena exist in music, painting, and prose, as noted.]

Mirror Image

Another set of clay tablets
Another flood
Drowning in water
Drowning in air
It's not enough to be mortal
It's not enough to be divine

He who saw the deep
Tamed thunder-hearted greed and lost
He who made the maze
Broke shame with flaxen thread and waxen wing
He who rose from the reeds to split the sea
Promised a land he'd never roam

They of plague and godly wrath
Surely we can reconcile ourselves to die
To cry from the lip of myth
                          ask
What is enough?
                    then live

[Gilgamesh, Daedalus, Moses all grappled with questions of destiny or free will.
It makes me wonder how we each decide what to live for, to die for.]

Quatrefoil
in memory of Allan Callow

Borderland triolet
Mother and two
Orbit an exile town
Tight-raft, hardihood, hurricane tape
Verbs without object noun

Arm in arm though a concrete grove
Crosswalk of heat-pummeled pavement
Each oscillates above a separate fraying point
Ground-quilt split at the seams

Assets disarrayed:
Horse of jade
Saddle of yak
Bound-foot slipper
Relics of conveyance
Working their weight

But as mother
Magnifies freeze-fractured traces
Distant ranges, riverbeds, delta of amethyst and opal

Moves wider to a land of Sabi sand
Where thorn tree and willow veld, marulo and mamba
Vie majestic and two stars embrace every corner of sky

The stars' source escorts her home
With warmth that won't scorch or stifle
Her two stars began too to glow

How could they know
It was written from the start
Embodied in the letters of his name
Four alike characters
Straight back, pointing the same direction
One enough for each
Essential to every living cell
L is for Love

[The title means four-leaf, as in a rare and lucky find. My stepfather died at age 99. He met my mother at a scientific conference in South Africa, and followed her home to meet my sister and me in Coconut Grove, Florida, He was a two-star admiral and esteemed vascular surgeon, but to us, he hung the stars. His name contains the letter L four times.]

Rothko Room at the Phillips Collection

I recall that very first time
Standing honest I don't know how
Legs arms slack-hinged
Interior space shuffled
Jewel-hung divisions
Replaced
What I used to call
Breath brushed
Not even the memory
Of anything before
Something more
Along the lines of lines of
Muddling, resolving
Passage of ash cloud
Maroon-rubbed sky
Embered umber orange
Green as alone
Blown blue wide
Crown of mind
Bending any hesitation to paragraphs
Passionate purpose seeming so beside the point
       I do recall   fear
             of missing it
Premonition of loss is still loss
Would I again
Pay attention
To that giant whisper?

It is only this morning
That I place it
Color signal
Of course
Your eyes

[I used to live near the Phillips in Washington D.C., and spent countless hours in the aura of Mark Rothko's paintings. Years later, I found that living glow looking back at me.]

La Pícara

Quiero palabras puras
La libertad de ideas fuertes
Trazos delicados
Quiero susurrar anhelos
Deseo con alas
Esparciendo sueños para cantar y encantar
Adentro todo
Cincos gotas de pintura
Bailar con sus respectivas andanzas
Y al centro de todo
Una tormenta arremolinada
Brisas del pirata
Ola el lienzo del mar

The Rogue

I need pure words
The liberty of strong ideas
Delicate traces
I want to whisper longing
Winged wish
Scattering dreams to sing and enchant
Within everything
Five drops of paint
Dance each with their own fates
And at the center of all
A swirling storm
Pirate breezes
Wave the canvas of the deep

The Clue to an Idle Inheritance

Years ago bent by glint
Of dust charged sunlight
Over hardback microscope
Detecting in novel's text
Each adult foible and folly
Unfolded, fixed, slide-mounted
Scotched by full transparency
Man-made mischief kid-cracked
Girl in the wide-banded head band
And me — Nancy Drew mentee —
Teeth cut on crime file titles
Sirens herald crossing stations
Tracks to my pilgrim soul
The Password to Larkspur Lane
The Sign of the Twisted Candles
The Secret of the Wooden Lady
Brave what may
Back to local library stack
Atheneum-cum-laboratory
Testing methods of literary discovery
Narrative, plot, character
So different my dissection
From my parents'
Flight muscle, insect, tissue, and lung
Clues I've never ceased sleuthing
Story arc, likely suspects, dead end theories
What we don't know
Always more than telling
What we answer for as so

[Josh Smith's photograph of a sidewalk crack prompted this poem. As a child, I spent much of my time in the library, wondering how I was related to my scientist parents. Differing styles of detection.]

S Curve

That which can be known
Flush with the unknowable
Pure ideal plumb to stickily human
Briefly such sweet symmetry
Breathed in plays, poetics, even politics
Found broke-perfect physical form
Within Aphrodite of Milos
Greek to her crystalline core though
Pedestalled in Paris under Roman name
Fusion complete as you
With arms seeking
Make hers harmonize
Body & Mind
And all unminding sets in motion
Rewind more mind unminding
Such gestures transfix
Lost arts and espials
Beauty bodied forth by
Fantastical familiar
Ours is not an age devoid of tragedy
Tuskless mammoth of Sesame Street
Mr. Snuffleuphugus
Once invisible to all but Big Bird
And we watchers sharing
The exquisite mystique of their company
When all is revealed
Certain sanctity is lost
Imagination flourishes best
Behind shaggy coat and luxuriant eye lash
Corners kept safe for make-believe friends

[A Josh Smith photograph of a drain pipe brought the Venus de Milo and Mr.
Snuffleuphugus into relief.]

Alchemy

Our last day
In the fallen garden
We'll build a bed of books
Epics nested edge to edge
Towering patchwork
Palaver of paradise lost and found
Tale-placed pitons
Test what heart can bear
Gathering bolt of allegory
Muse metered rope
Naked we scale
Just human heights
Your fingers stitched in mine
Enact the act itself
Spool of blood and sweat
A laboring love wet with centuries
Who will tell us thus
    How to be
    The meaning of all touch
Surrender story in animal service
To forgotten faith
As the drowning forget the feeling of thirst
Traverse blazing bower
Voices melt
Into one golden line
Once upon a time

"Of night and light and the half-light"

That corner
Dusk coming on
   Fast over floor
Common breath at last
     Instantly becoming
My Favorite   everything
 My Favorite (fill in the blank)
I'm even stealing your lines now
Lost is the voice of alone
   the not filled feel of alone
(In flight above city sidewalk
 carpet of leaves, sapphire and ruby
   gilded collar, cigarette casing
    day's descent across cheek to mouth)
Re-enter, return
To that corner
Rereading Oscar Wilde
 "The Happy Prince"
   Finery stripped
   Nothing left but leaden heart
   Conscript swallow cold at his feet
Realizing the final lines
Enfolding what is most precious
At the end of all
Those perfect lines
Are absolutely
Also
Yours

[The title comes from a line in W.B. Yeats' "He Wishes for the Cloths of Heaven".]

Not to Diminish

for Matt Gonzalez

Though we spoke
Only of a poem
I must have known
Some day
All my verse
Would condense
Into one

You returned
The intimacy
Of your shoe against mine playful
Are you nervous?
Excited, I replied
I must have known
The way you knew my jacket would be returned
The way you held my hand
The way you know people are good
They just get lost

Are you friendly? asked the woman
Seeking direction on a down-market street
This became your query to me
What was I before?
I am learning a new language
Remapping geography
Unbundling nerves
Switch-wired words that can't find my tongue

Abstractions, wild gestures
Like the paintings
You show me how to see
Rise to my lips
I lick them all-over impasto
Each stroke an active transmission
Because even I love you
Diminishes
This inconceivable
Lithification of lyric and limb

Are we lucky?
You tease
As I reach for more
Of the speechless story
Our bodies make
Must keep making
One
Yes
To grow
And keep growing

Shadow of the Waxwing

Speakeasy

Muse,
Have I been wearying your storefronts with my wares
Displacing native nuance with ornamental flair?
Forgive my frippery
May we decree
Our jungle will not be gentrified
By posh pretense or cult muffin
Let us traffic as leopards
Eminent in our private domain
All I ask is occasional leave
To enter you as you do me
Flaming vines across drawbridge
Rungs lit with musk-lantern
Wet words
Dotting fur
Limbering lawless limbs
Dip under canopy
Spring over understory
Marking territory
Spot on spot

Dart

Candescent before a mirror
The bare silhouette of a girl
Measures the full length
Of another flat day

Past window pane
Beyond the torpid tangle
Of heat and hesitation
A figure rises
Essential as an angel sprung

Carving air, impossibly light
A boy within resplendent wings
Shapes order
With wax, paper, reed

I exist
She thought
To bear witness

-/-

In a farther room
Her father looks up from his work bench
Rough assemblage of levers, forceps, gears

Setting aside mothers of invention
His hands lift and bend
To shield the sun

Back-lit the body in flight
Now perceptible
Clouds his known world

The mind of man
Must know its place
He thinks
An archer keeps to range

-/-

As evening
Rolls its fire
Across the outcast plain
A flock of wild birds gathers

Circling the arrow
Whose sharp nib had found
Then requited
Mass to ground

They fly
Disarranging make-believe
Feathers
Against the crumbled body

Faster they wheel
As if
Once more
To propel

Soft form
Gateless sway
Her turn
Into flight

[This poem reworks Daedalus and Icarus' wax-singed flight, with a twist for
Ariadne in the mix. In Greek mythology, there are various and often opposing
versions of all the great legends. It's a reminder that we write our own endings.]

Shadow of the Waxwing

Her life had become
Punctuated equilibrium
A dream to station oscillation
The seasonless sky still seldom bore rain
But from time to time a tear appeared
Blink-blot of a boy
Brushing the blistered clock-face of the sun

-\-

She'd grown accustomed to this
Recovered from the shock
Of watching the first
In perfect flight
Sliced by an arrow
Drawn by a father now long-dead

His workshop
Had become her foundry
She pressed his wicked tools
Into witness
Shaped contrivances
Of useful finery
From memory

Readying her kit
For those sky-split moments
When she'd fasten her contraption
Cry *"Teach me"* at a run
To the bird-boy aerial umbras
Her gold-flashed arms scoped
To stroke the flame

-\-

Transfixed by
Delicate tracery
They would fall towards her
Voice and filigreed frame

Parachuting
Salvation
Or repair

For whom
On aerofoil feathers
Hovering
Each learned
Part by part
The gossamer art
Of current and glide

The melt felt slipstream
Of terrestrial dawn
Appendage and extremity
Synchronized
In wiper-wide circumference
Swept into earth and
            forever   visible from space

[This verse can be read as a sequel to "Dart". The line comes from the opening
of Vladimir Nabokov's novel *Pale Fire*: I was the shadow of the waxwing slain /
By the false azure in the windowpane / I was the smudge of ashen fluff — and I /
Lived on, flew on, in the reflected sky."]

Windsworth

A train ride's journey past patch-work fields
Plots thatched and brindled
Green-laddering thoughts of plucked
Wild berry, lashes of ginger beer and licorice
The all-knowing aroma of buttered biscuits
Lying warm on wool within
A careful line of saxon roses
Taking turns to read aloud of puma and the river dwellers
I suspect its closeness to *pluma* brought the picture of a feathered
Creature to mind's eye
I can't help but still imagine tropical colors
Charging its fur-lined coat at full speed
Back then books
Told their own tales
I recall the time I cried
To see the Hobbit projected on the silver screen
Looking nothing like the one I'd dreamed
Eye-level with toad stools, blowing wishes to launch lady birds
Off skinny thighs east-born to the sea
I have scant memory
Of being truly young
Always looking after you
As I am now wishing
You'd come round that garden gate
Shy as a school boy
Holding the notes of my name
Like a secret
Worth sharing

[Memories of lying on the lawn with my father reading *The Wind in the Willows*
at his parents home in Eastbourne, on England's south coast. The name of their
house gives the poem its title.]

The Collector

in memory of David Spencer Smith

From you I wouldn't learn
How to change a tire
Balance accounts
Enter a room
Belong
Yours were lessons for another age
Time travelers
We skirted indigenous zones
Storm-cleared spits of sand
Mangrove marsh & thrumming grove
Places populated by insect antiquity
Even our home lodged an unpeopled past
Chinese ceramics colonized shelves
Like distant cousins squinting
Under dynastic glaze (early Sung)
Or through impossibly thin-walled intricacies
Of Qing-blue phoenix and Celadon dragon
Every table a pedestal for foreign objects
Butterflies by provenance pinned
Beetles with pharaoh-wise eyes
Abed rolls of cotton wool
Also cowrie shells and square-holed coins
Chunks of mixed metal incused
With characters you'd decrypt with care
I knew I'd never cinch the detail
Just impressions of the scene:
Within one faint smudge
Two see-through argonauts

me:
   scared little lotus lost among the cranes
   translucent to the point of vanishing

you:
   with net raised
   intent on some prized find

Lo: how I wished to sky out
And be caught

Gato

"all cats were lions once," Jack Micheline

The downtrodden saint was right
On the cradle state of cats
Root roar crouched in purr
Concealed weapons tucked
In paw poised to swipe
And yet
We coax them into bed
Sixth sense subdued
Lapped numb
By sandpaper tongue
Downy fur standing
Feral self on end
Claws-climb teeth-test rough-reflex
Once bitten
Twice shy
We are all just
Waiting to be
Untamed

Field Recordings

Licked fingers
Whet the crystal
Edge dialing
Honey wink
Sound buzz
Brim and shoulder
Blade crushed
Grape and grass
Nocturne
Tuned to
Round song

Still Life

Spread out on
Sheets of canvas
Mouth full of caution colors
          & hurricane intention
Cape-cloth rubbing
Pit from fig and grape
Tubes of oil topless
Oozing improper
Proportions puddling
SubjectObjectOccasion

Massing
Prime-felt
Still-wet
To touch
& still
So much more than
Life like

Lucid Dream

Cupboards and closets
Contain for most
Baggage of excesses
Coats that never kept us warm
Potions for cleaning up messes

But the simplest
Doors and drawers
In your home
Preserve what
I can't live without
Clay,
       paper,
            glue,
(I should want less)
                  Waking with you

An Arc for the Frozen Sea

When the only forbidden answer
To a genie offering three wishes
Is made moot by biomedicine and machine
We won't need the one wily grant
                — for endless more —
To implant
Leisure without limit
Elixirs to erase old traces
Disease, sorrow, loss effaced
From collective memory
A settling selflessness left
When we delete request
Bad files on war and such
We could even wish only to see in 10-D
All expansive possibility and pattern recognition
Soul mates without dictum of face, form, or race
This may be our fate
— At present
We mortals are neither within nor without
A gate is dissolving
At the threshold writhes a dusty carapace
Avatar of Kafka's dying wish
That all he ever wrote be burned unread
Oblation to the angels of his imagination
He felt he failed by base execution
For us for now
Greatness still lies
In unappeasability

What abides
Is the wish
And this :
We tried
We altered
We chose

The Dude
for Charles Scully on his 15th Birthday

If Rudyard Kipling covered
The unforgiving minute
With 60 seconds of resilience 101
I give you:
Name that one-hit-wonder
Cussing at cards
Odes to baseball
T-shirts to faded rockers
Arguments on Xerxes
Oh and Homer — Doh!
I didn't know
How to raise a son
Just knew I wanted you
And now it's clear
15 years of ordering
"Ossom butt cheeks"
Isn't going to win me a Pulitzer
But it might have been enough
To remind you to feel loved
And keep on
Wise one baking
Heart's hundred dozens of
Chocolate Bacon Donuts
You have a shining sword
To share those winnings
      Brush your teeth
      Abide
I bow to the exceptional person you are
(And that's not just, like, my opinion man)

[My son is a great fan of the Cohn Brothers' existential drama "The Big Lebowski", hence some of the references.]

Figuration

Our first winter weeks
Out of the box
Cinnamon dizzy crowds
Navigate their ribboned packages past
The window where we glide
Cursive strokes of axel and arabesque
Crazy eights electrified by
Precise parallel legs
Arms always stretched

How many turns did we make believe
For the bake shop fogged by coffee and waking
Magnetic feet flying over faux-frozen pond?

Superstitious of endings
I was afraid to count
Sure the day would come
As it did
The pair of us packed away
For another holiday's display
Leaving us to sort the lineation
Of a new season
Adjusting eyes to interior light
We sort unfamiliar shapes
Welcome lengthier pleasures
Bodies pressing at last
Inclination into weight
Gravity guiding the infinite
Loop upon loop

[When we first met, my love would send video snippets of a holiday window display from a nearby bakery. When the season changed, I found myself wondering about the pair of mechanical skaters and how they were getting on.]

The Machinery of the World is too Complex

The years will catch us
Before we let go chasing
All cryptic imprints evaporate
A pageant of tidal sunsets
Stubborn scholar scratchings
Snippets — the conversations we will never have again

Can you imagine freezing
Life's frame long enough
To confirm hints that a force or fact
Impractically essential persists
Surrenders certainty to the futility of regret
Forgives our base need to affirm potency
However scant

Such as — that line by Verlaine
The blind scholar on the park bench
Could not recall
Forgotten and yet not forgotten
Lying like a wayward lacuna
Warm on a distant rock
Blissfully unaware of the hunt

How unlike the we who await instruction
Hoarding hope specter to breast thought
Straining to hear
The smallest part of you
Whisper *may this too survive*

[The title and some of its touchstones come from Jorge Luis Borges.]

June 4

Immediacies of 3am
Ardent asseverations
Inside the icicle hour
Second hand falling
            as light through lace
Golden ray verging
Up the opal face
Tick tock
Idle knock of shaken sound
It's self-wound a distant voice decries
By way of account
We resume in doubt
Some stable gear may have slipped
            yes/and
Is that a fault
Slipping ?
Thumb and finger
Hinge into decision
Rest or resume
Participles strung in non-finite form
                    sensation before articulation
                        Latin variant literally
                        "a sharing, partaking,"
                            expressing
                    both noun and adjective
Por ejemplo: let us assume ourselves
Two seals at play
Rolling/rolled
Holding/held
Never far from infinitive
Closely conjugated
Slipping
Yes/and
Laced

[A birthday poem. Year one. I did have his watch fixed. There are two seals].

Within Hesitation

Should I tell you
No
I shouldn't
I've already
Told you
I'd said my last no
Back then
Before I'd said
My first yes
The issue is not the
No but the telling
The missing of
The could of
That moment
The again wanting
To feel
You not knowing
What you
Now always
Know the mystery
Of the answer
Was never
In question
I should
Not
Ask it
Again
But
Yes
Do

Fugue

I cannot tell you
What to do
How to think
Or what to say
I cannot quantify how to be
Draw lines around emotion
Map the right response
Or teach you trust
I am weak
Frequently wrong
Full of fearsome freedoms
Famished by faith
Hiding dread in both hands
Conscious that minute vibrations
Keep time
Mouthing
Slowly
There is a pace to all things
This earth is never mute
I am not afraid to cry
Sorrow of seas
Let us long
To howl
To sing

Abacus of Right Action

Here's the lowdown on Heroism
How much easier it is when a monster
Tall on terrible legs starts swallowing ships
Or invaders swarm the village torches blazing
The reptile brain needn't factor odds
When it's our fate encircled by rabid dogs

Truth is Brute
Instinct not Bravery
Authors most epic feats
Reason luxuriates in the labyrinthine
Multi-tined trajectories forking myriad probable paths
Auger of rabbit holes not moral math

Between *I ponder* and *I do*
Lies the fall
Logic struggles to compute
      Plight of strangers
      Systemic flaw
      Inequity of existing law
Against our own catalogue of fears
Portion of comfort

How much harder it is
To bear the steady drip of human travail
Measuring mercy on a sliding scale
Mine versus yours
Ours versus theirs
Marooned and grasping

Safety ropes we don't know how to throw
All I know – words – my tow line through time
Try these: *Grain by grain, branch by branch, being by being*
History hails the grand campaign
But Nature moves in multiples
A ceaseless determined quiet shifting

And so, the lowdown on Doing : 1+1+1
      Grain by grain, branch by branch, being by being

In the ecology of action
Lies the leap
      Finch's beak
      Peppered moth
      The moray eel's extra jaw
Proof that behavioral alteration
Breeds new patterns

So forget finding an algorithm for just
How and when to change this world
Move a bead across the row
     with those you love
             those you'll never know

Consider your life   theirs

    Add a bead

          You   do   the math

Daily Grind

laid out across your bed
i'm a speed bump on the way
to your first cup of coffee
every morning
curled up
center of
sugar lump
stirring you
every way
into morning
cup to saucer
bump across
bed edge
center jump
speed mate
melting
morning
very very
yours yours yours

Pentimento

What trace will remain
Of our weapon-toothed race
When we too are supplanted?

Painted-over plots surfaced
By the transparency of time
Confessions unsealed and encased
In amber facture of desert haze
Each vain stroke of conquest
Scratched upon the naked slate of the earth
Under trace of human will
Faded from paper, canvas, silicon, film
Dust to dust
All but this
Constellation of regret
Pocked by sand stared shapes
The outlines of lost sailors
Ourselves
      Pirates so long
           We raid our own vessels
               Night after night

Is this our fate?

Grown mad
Deaf to the mineral silence of salt
Blind to animations of
Air fire water
Dumb to the ageless
Lesson of the soil
Ground is given

Not to prove
But to grow

[This poem was inspired by the photography of David Maisel. His images of human destruction and neglect, such as nuclear proving grounds, are stunning and harrowing.]

Libertad o Sacrificio?

in memory of Radcliffe Squires

Man of craters and caverns
Carpels and caltrops
I can almost believe
You'd have looked upon
Her mirror-hand of writhing snakes
To efface the paradox of self-pretense
Why we always enter gardens
But never emerge
Except from sleep or sky
Tempted by what's been lost
Forgetting we hid it there ourselves
Ardor, of course, being
The first thing we learn
To transgress
So I look carefully without you knowing
Reliving a moment I didn't share
That day in the square I wanted to ask
Was it you who called Medusa the first sculptor
Slipped
Sunlit paws
Under islands
Casting lake-like reflections at flat metal seas
Promising grandeur in the unfinished
Spinning each thread as though your could tempt
Mythic gold back into neutral human straw
Spool just enough slack
To slant through
Passages of notorious consequence
That we might
Return
Stone softened
Straw winged
Burning with ardor

[Radcliffe Squires was a poet, who had almost been forgotten. I built a Wikipedia page to preserve and promote his memory. Happily, a volume of his collective verse, edited by Donald Beagle, has been published to mark the centennial of his birth.]

50 Ways

for Jack Hirschman and Agneta Falk

All those Eskimo words for snow
Such linguistic lavishing
When undressed
Reveals a marvel
Of promiscuous metonymy
That is not romantic excess
But grammatical vigor
Those encoded polysyllables serve as seed source
Suffix after suffix coupled to stem
Breeding sentences full of meaning
Between lips sealed flush
So single word-buds ripen on the tongue

— with such precious cargo
it's no wonder they kiss
mouth closed rubbing noses —

How heady the exactitude of their urgency
Life and death distinctions
Secrets of a frozen landscape waved as
Scarf bright warnings
To signal snow's mood-multiples:
"fragile as crystal"
"drifts you fall into"
"snow that closes eyes"
"powder packed hard enough to cross"

What flag do we raise
As *snow* to Eskimo
Sand to ancient Pharaoh?

Spirits move their periscope
Chests across the inlets
Of this chosen bay
Where submarine sky
Out spies its own disguise
Denudes presumption
By arcane anthem
Beats that push the tide

In fog : fragile
In fog : fallen
In fog : precious
In fog : rubbing

The Tassel of St. J

It was never about the red hat
Or the tombs of other saints
The wanderer knelt for the knowledge
Of pagan scholars
The perfect solitude of vellum
The flesh-trembling transmutation
Of ink into everything
Bound beyond book cover
Anthologies of animal anguish
Aches that wrest wild thorn
Free with lip bidden
To pant all-foured
On hieroglyphs of sand
Certain there is no desert
No test nor text no lesson
It was never about the red hat
It was always about the lion

[Jerome was a saint of earthly devotions, a scholar and historian, who took time
from his studies to care for an injured lion.]

Crackerjack

Ends fray
Threads split
Even as we try
To fit each bit back
The whole won't hold

There is an ebb to old openings
Silt built grit year on year
Narrows (it would appear)
The fundamental line
Can not move through

So it unspools
The toy beads scatters
To corners and grooves
It's almost comical
The way we begin to chase
"I" over there
"You" yonder
And the central piece
In faded letters "Love"

We reach out
At the same time
Each capturing the memory
Of sticky discovery
The present that rises to the top
Of the box
As the prize

By Feigned Remoteness

How is it you see me?
Serene passerine
Satin gloss and trailing tail

False azure's a feint
I see which side of the sky tilts up
When I hit the pane

Clear
As the conscience
Of meltwater

Vertical
Free fall
Waxing

Witness
Obstacle transformed
To assignation

[Passerines are a common species of bird, which includes the waxwing.]

Duende

for Mark degli Antoni

How many nights
For blood or surrender
He rowed the coast
Of twilight to lay feet
Flamenco-hard upon ivory tile
Unsettling bets with fists
Of scrambled wire
Scaling bare-soled fault scarps
Scared by forgotten splendor
Years caught stealing glances
At the bronze ghost
Roiling a brushstroke sea
Chariot horse tricks
Drilling confession from the gloom
Holding the echo
Of the gull's cry
Like a rein
Tight but loose

Cut-Up

In truth, the recording angels are neither seraphim nor cherubim. All celestial accounts are settled by a volunteer squad of fortune tellers and bookies This rag-tag band of chimerical charlatans lurk Pearly Gate-side primed to cross amulets across the black box of your existence. They assemble what remains of your flight among the living. Evidence of accidents and incidents laid out like yard-sale offerings; someone gets the boom-box going, nectar flows, and well, it gets pretty pogo from there. Can you imagine, slam-dancing with all those swirling scarves?

Anyhow, the net-net is this: what's left of your story lies in strewn wreckage way more messy than the spectacle of Humpty Dumpty's worst acid trip. And the morning-after is basically all about dustpans and glue pots, inside jokes, and yet more free-for-all shots of ambrosia. Finally, the re-jiggered curios of a souvenir life are displayed with great fanfare in a glass vitrine. You look, in a word, intriguing. At last!

But here's the thing: all your secrets have remained safe. Yours to keep in perpetuity. An eternal mystery that outlives all efforts to the contrary.

Exhibit A: Her greatest wish
                    Her deepest fear

Bare Lines

Center Ring:
Head vs. Heart

How might I
Without whip
Or cane chair high
Coax you to calm?

Obstinate beast
I long to reach
Some soft point
Of entry where
We play untrained
Without applause
Brawl or guard
The mind of me
Swallowed
Headless into yours
So we can't think
       to tarry
           to taste
               the lees
                   the legs
                       the long finish

Quixote

What was the windmill
To make of your jousting
It's as comic a scene as this
Sunset flanked giant
Turned towards
Your charge
Just iron visor
Piercing the pellicle of
Illusory air's embrace
Assailed in the very act
Of revolution
Arms reeling
And all
Stolen kisses
Out blown as
Emptied wishes

A Very Good Journey

in memory of Leonard Cohen

& that was that was that
You broke
The first and only rule
No leaving
Before looking to the sea
Call your soul flared
Lighthouse home
To the island of springs
And ancient astronomy
Making very good
Use of water planting
Tears to tear tears away
Away with you then
All your messages
Came through
A line of love has dropped
In dimming surrender
The barbarians of our nature
Have arrived
It's almost too much
But what times we had
& time it is
To set out
Upon the water
Be not afraid
For the rays of the sun
Will stand at attention
With laurel crown and cypress forest
Rare perfume
Fresh joys
Await
& our soft eyes

[Leonard Cohen lived for some time on the Greek Island of Hydra.]

Ars Poetica

Release this roseate girl blush
Too muchness of speech
From her lacquered layered
Decoupage veil
Toss off the camouflage rhetoric
This is not an age of patience
We make haste with the chaste
Prolong only just so long
The exact moment
Of becoming
Ineffable
Drifting dandelion
Unclasped by cloud
Captured in the coup
Of surrender

Amid a Crowd

Come stranger
We've been years
In the sweet
Stay of slack tide
Unstressed by ebb or flow
Slant-set drift nets
Outside time's arrow
Buoyant as coins
Tossed with no score to settle
Sheer-float signal souls
Bound by bracketed intimacy
Two figures
Nearing recall
On either side of waterfall
Followed by storm watch
Punctuator of all
Separate returns
Always and never
Returns re-turned
Seized from the day
You ceded my bard's
Glowing bars back
To me murmuring
How you live here now
(touches self)
No line bare

Bringing It All Back

an homage to Bob Dylan

Epoch of the paper map
When time and place
Folded awkwardly upon resolve
We learned to pick quickly
Coast forward
Never straight
It still works this way
Blink and you miss
Exits looking
Back
That falling flash-card
Is no benign
Highway sign
The ramp's slick
The curve blind
Look out kid
Let's see what you did

-/-

Certain tracks tap
Me back to Philly
Staring at the statue
(Then on-set at the Spectrum)
Of the famous boxer
Title belt in a sea of tie-dye traffic
Atlas arms exalted
Mine too but ungloved
Chin high contender
Felling young for once
About being grown up
Such as not fretting
How to get
To the next show
Or where to stay in Roanoke
So many maturely amateurish
Adventures to recount
Soundtrack of my-fidelity
With audible rapport
Tied all these years later

To those songs
It wasn't even he
I was there to hear
The Other Ones
Plus Jerry live
Covered you
Then later that night
At someone's cousin's place
A stranger handed me a ticket
Or left it in my shoe
Then it was you centering
An airy amphitheater
Solitary figure
Lyrical trigger
Shadow in a circle-spell
Chanting at the inner ear
Your hum-loud hymns
I couldn't catch
A single word
Tangled up
Nor wanted to

-/-

The needle of the mind
Drops its considerable weight
On patterned grooves
We begin even to sing erstwhile
Scratches into sequence
As comfort from suspense
Perhaps there
Between the chorus
Lines trapped in time
Another anthem plays
For the little boys lost
Not Fade Away

-/-

But hope refracts
Vinyl cracks
As a fragile
Relic

A confidence
Dropped
We do so love
Riven sound
More than
Humming alone
Capitulation
Lifts lines to a given crest
Hangs the precise moment
Of loss
Before & after
So we hear every crack
Test inevitable shattering
By holding itself together
Just one more breath
If not for you

-/-

At last I approach
With no idea
Only sad appetite
And splendid song
Neither of which
(Laughable, I am told)
Can be expressed
Oh, I have forgotten the circumstance
Of this sleepless remembrance
But by light of a basement reel
Footage makes frontage
Nests within
The broken melody
Of someday
Returning
Ungloved
A bird that flew

[After Dylan won the Nobel Prize, I hosted a poetry dinner with "Dylan" as the writing prompt. I struggled to get his lyrics and tunes out of my head, so that my own could take shape. Finally, I focused on memories from a Grateful Dead tour that intersected with other youthful escapades, including an unexpected Dylan show.]

Marble Warrior

for Mary Julia Klimenko

as in all things
pulling against

or leaning to
desire is severed

like a limb or a head
the pit of the statue

reworked or remounted
regardless anew

metamorphism being
rock's first luster

interlock of impure
pressure polished to vein

and waxy scar
sobs sculpted without face

calm polished
compared to me

restless with cigarette packets
covered in verse

modern tar coated couplets
crumbled and corked in bottles

tossed to cross a white sea
art glass toys

rolling frail ransom
to the breach

[Mary Julia is a marvelous poet and a very dear friend. For over 40 years, she was
the model and muse to sculptor Manuel Neri. His tools were chisel and ax. Ours
are words and the forms that they make and remake.]

Poseidon's Lament

Cold obstinate vapor
Take off that coat of armistice
You know of no more news from nowhere
No one would kneel by such brooding
Pools of blank self-countenance
Clutching the belly of a ram
To sheer off how many
Have been consumed
Spelling sins of sentiment in ragged letters
— loyal oyster vesicant elegy —
At such cost
Lain over vain embers
Trail fog-spent rescue
Down twinned peaks
Tracks where there is no third rail
And a hissing speaker indicates
You must collect your baggage
And begin the hard return
Through the gloom
To abandoned avenues
Where spindrift laughter
Claims an unlabeled valise
As found

[Once walking in the outer avenues of San Francisco late at night, we passed an abandoned suitcase. What would have happened had we looked inside?]

A Bene Placito

If I could palm my way into
The glove of your sleeping self
You might see the literal
Heart of me flash
Immodest embassy
Because this is how I arrive
Like an acquacious animal
Shedding raiment
Like a too-tight shell
Like a white flag
Wrapped to a mast
Like a dove denuded
Cooing for peace
With pen
In place of branch
Drawing pearls
From cyclone spools
To string a night
Paced by frisbee moon
Its lunar phases lifting
Your waking face
A shimmering oasis
There
Could be no more
Perfect moment
Than this

Sleepwalker

Sift in silence
Down the milky column of
Moth occulted midnight
The crooked fable will fork
To cobblestone runway
Sink to a carpet of poppies
Stem split by a preordained polarity
Each side swinging
Asynchronous
Dutch doors unlatched
An opposition akin to
Two hands missing
An intended meeting
Loose itinerant icebergs
Paroled but purposeless
Such requisite debt
Is known in the bone
It forms the frame
As only one hand
Can another
Affix the arris
Shape the sharp edge
Between surfaces
So from dreams
We may safely pass

365 Lightening Strikes

It was your ritual of home
Scenes in motion
Long before this year
Of changing
Art from place to place
Making room
Takes more than
Good eyes
Or arms to hang
Moments of emptiness
Between spoken words
Drawn lines
Calm in light
Bright in wait
Brush and wood
Working discovery
In any position
We both were
Born to the sign of air
Ruled by mind
Mutable or fixed
Thoughts mixed
Will never over fill
And this is why
Time itself expands
Weightless within
Skin on skin
Days upon days
Exquisite balsam
The way we move
Each other's walls around

Three Rivers Returning

The muse
Anything
But seated
Plaster only
As the kind
That heals
Says write
Three lines
A day on a day
When another
Keeper of word wonder
Cites an old world tradition
Of asking the most helpless thing
For protection from grave menace

We must share secrets sayings such as these
For humanity cannot keep its own promises
Call the poets up — enlist
We volunteer army of three
Ballading ghost fire
To a cold-eared pond
We shall stir the reeds
The way a child turns
An empty pocket out
To free any possibility
That we may again
With sweetness
Fill our cheeks
Enough to attest
Lorca,
We crickets
Are marching

[I wrote this poem after exchanging notes with two other poets, Mary Julia Klimenko and Beau Beausoleil. The world needs more such creatures.]

Eros Epicentered

One sits
Here on
Window watch
Where trumpet vines
Offer water witching
To eager wasps
Divining then diving
Body-rod into flared petal
Bell nectar bobbing
With immodest intention
(Oh) & how lovely to be so
Literal speaking of nature
Without rouging the mention
With circuitous reserve
And beveled indifference
For one loses
So much behind
The skirts of indefinite pronouns
— each, another, many, same —
Pretending pleasure isn't
An extractive industry
Mining
Being an acquisitive word
Ought also to mean
Made mine
By act of drawing
Desire ichor-dear
To telluric self-center
Bellybutton bubbling
Molten emotion

Trembling oracle
Peel thyself
Laughter shaking
A known gibberish
Free and (Oh)
Such classicism
From the naked
Surfer girl

[The Oracle at Delphi was considered by the ancient Greeks to be the *omphalos*, literally the navel or center of the world.]

Lullaby

You
With the curb kicked
Root ripped
Reeling heart
Keep tumbling
Your way
Bawling right
Past claptrap
Sooth all sophistry
Sage preened philosophy
Time will come to be worldly
Feel very free for now
To say "sod off"
Busking poet
Save the trope
Set your tombstone
Afloat
So it may sink and rise
   & you
    stormy
    glassy
   sinking and rising
   rocking to rise
   & you
   smooth as can be
   skiping thorns
   like rocks
   across the summer lull
   smoothed as a page turned
   you
   like the surface of the sea
   glass shadowy
   as night tucks her thorns
   softly into roses

Chaconne

      Glowing grain glorious
As a luthier's splendid
Soundboard spruce
Cut on the quarter
Matched to maple's
Curling flame
& together-wise harmonized
Two-ply well-nigh human sigh
A threshed sigh shaking
Sensation free of sentiment

Say, can you relate
As I do
These transcendent tones
To what feels farther than what we utter
When you warm wood
Soothe sweet beams
Between my corrugated pleats
Sides, ribs, and neck
Thrum beckon with
Ground bass bow
Bending willow in tonic service
Willing sonic conduit
Up to pierce the mantle
Of diamantine darkness
Sharp tongue rapid
Semitones unfurling like petals

Strum seanced instrument
We were made to form
This perfecting choir

A Nest for Shiny Objects
lines composed at Freestone Ranch

We are back in this place of rabbit warrens and running hills. Dark broad birds dance high above the storm-beaded branches. They tease the air like matadors. But this spectacle of prancing body-capes is even too much drama. We're here for sweet ease. So our jokes twist-off easier than a drunk on a bar stool. That one about the nosey neighbor never gets dry. And speaking of Tom Waits, our little stable of rocking horses have been drinking since dawn. They need a rub down and you need a bubble bath. Bring the wine. I ache in hard to get places.

Tub drunk, smiling to myself, vapored by this most happy caesura. I close my eyes to recall you in the sure candor of your effortless morning's self-possession, which I think is really your natural state. Your face lifts from art-making, hands follow, and I remember back to when you pretended to worry I wouldn't like them. I pretend now not to worry, which is in fact my natural state. And from here those hands only seem more bright than the birds in the sky from which I had to turn away. Do you know that I've kept that cropped series of photos you sent — your hands gesturing, your hands at rest, your hands waiting to be led. Let me show you. This way. It's time for bed.

All Things Considered

Your accented voice modulates the radio. And everything near me.

Leaning, I imagine you, to keep from falling.

Whoever we are, wherever we are, we are always up against whatever else remains.

As separate lives go, sameness sits in atoms alone. But as you hold me from afar by your words, I know you better than those passing on the road, careless in their casual comforts.

You are in me like a spine.

They took your father. Your brother, your neighbors, your home. They took your proud city and its alleys. Parks. Poems. People. So much swept litter.

Sideways in a shed without a roof, You lie blinking at the sky. One need not disbelieve in time or distance to find our eyes meet.

Together we follow as they gather, memories unique but coefficient, fueled as fire drinks air.

The short interview with you, young man, is nearly over. Yet you've fanned the ashes of cold news and my cold heart. You were speaking of a bird in a cage. One possession that hadn't been destroyed. You'd been asked about hope. *Do you still have it?*

Of course, you said. *Because, the bird.*

In the country where I live, people speak of freedom as escape. But you hold it on your lap. The warmth of your inner world soothing hope through filagree reeds as a mother's ribcage held the first dream of you.

The dogs are loose on the darkling plain.

But you are the wind. You the flame.

You because you. The bird.

[Written to mark the 10 year anniversary of the bombing of Al-Mutanabbi Street Baghdad's ancient district of booksellers and literary cafes.]

"How is it that you live, and what is it you do?"

The tree is a sponge
The earth a sponge
& what are we ?
with skin
porous like bark
lungs that breathe
as coral reef

Shall we be babes in the bath
Freed by the loosening grace of water
Lushening our terraced hearts to hanging gardens
We'd see all surface stippled with countless iridescent worlds
Lift each glinting bubble of maybe to eye level
And blow it forward with a wish

Or let's be gypsies in formation
Wind our serpentine shadows across the spiny ground
Blend with the borderless caravan of stars
Never heading their way nor ours
So by wagon wheel we'll spin the agate eye of destiny
Upon the backward-facing view
Imagining the dust of our thoughts
Rearrange the sky

there is value in the waiting place
where ideas get space
but by the by
make no mistake
there is no peace in escape
for fate is the shell
we carry
on our backs
its weight is reckoned
by the life
we grow

the choice is ours
to despair our lot
or gloat in gain or fame

but what of this — we could persist
like the leech gatherer on the lonely moor
though old and poor
not declaiming talent or luck
just gathering
what's essential
releasing what is not

each day
not an end
but an outset
a call to press on
and keep pressing
beyond pause or applause
for we make what we are
when we don't just take
what we're given
but create
what we give

each day
not an end
but an outset
a reset
in-breath-out
so you may be persistent
with your art, your instrument, your invention,
your hands and your heart, your mind and your voice

it is never too late
for I loved that 5th symphony
but, ah, bright wings
what of the 9th

tireless, tested,
scared (even deaf)
we reset greatness
to make sense beyond sound

permeable
trued
recenter your colony
reenter yourself
wring out, fill up
don't quit

The tree is a sponge
The earth a sponge
And you
How is it that you live
What is it you do

[The title is a line from William Wordsworth's "Resolution and Independence" and 'bright wings' is sampled from Gerald Manley Hopkins.]

Standing Figures

By chisel born
A moan of shock
Shakes the rock
Laughing with dust
And release from form

Voids contain
Their own
Sculptural presence
A boring through to possibility
A channeling out
Opaque to bright

Nature may abhor a vacuum
But creates them all the time
Nicking chinks
For new energy to show
We are the stones that the river wears
Pearls polished smooth
Then drilled through
By riffles of rough water
Bearing legends
Like stones threaded
Carried or worn it is said
To ward off evil

Ancestors hung them from bedposts
So that now
Swaddled in our own fates
Spells strung
From all four corners
We turn from suffocation
Slough off our isolation

Stand up
To open
As gates do
A framed view
Though costal arch

The positive space
Of ocean swells
And everywhere sails
Braced to windward
Saluting many more
Suns beyond

Genesis

Under homespun cover
Things not visible
Impress the more
By their lack of need
To merchandize the unexplored

Regard the vast buttressed
Iridescent artistry
Of red abalone
Which occurs internally
Or at least within

His hinged shell of home
Or hers whose domed contours
Capture —what
Vast Sistine cravings
We can only guess

Their baroque devotion
Biomineralized
Distilled to abstraction
Sea -/- sky cloud -/- bed
Crystallized

Choreography
Ruffle tongue leaning
To lobe -/- muscle
volcada
 (ergo lingo
reserved for nacre confession)

Spiral-spoken supplications
— here is the chapel
— here the steeple
Hearts hidden at the apex
Of otherworldly ceilings

Fingers near-touching
In the beginning
We lit nights
End to end
Like chain smokers

WHERE DO WE COME FROM / WHERE ARE WE / WHERE ARE WE GOING

Don't say we're done
Run out of wonder we

Turquoise & sarcoline
Mikado & wenge

Synthetizers of spectrum we
Optionalize intertwinement

Draw the lark of lush
Delight from the throat of twilight

— red / yellow / blue —
— see / feel / do —

Weaving primary values we
Wreath of afterglow's uttering

Orange, violet, green
   que te quiero

Cinnebar, laurel, lavender
Honeybee wavelength offspring hues

Ingenious & uncoded
We'll be light transmission

Throb translation
Transiting the mortal eye

As wish / as want / as love
   que te quiero

[A research scientist trained a neural network to generate new paint colors,
complete with appropriate names. She concluded: "1. The neural network really
likes brown, beige, and grey; 2. The neural network has really, really bad ideas
for paint names." The poem's title comes from a painting by Paul Gauguin. The
Spanish phrase "que te quiero" echoes Gabriel Garcia Lorca's ballad to green,
and translates as "how I love you" or "how I desire you".}

Floodplain

In the season of the pollywog
An army of amphibians stationed its forces
At a pond behind my childhood home
Embedded with the troops (self-appointed scribe)
I'd log their calendrical metamorphosis
In a 3-ring binder
The way a mom
Pencils the height of her brood
Up the kitchen wall

At this wholly aquatic life stage
Tadpoles cycle first in cotillion
Globular blobs twitching spindly tail rudders
Until (days-on) thin extremities straighten their wake
Delicate and obvious
Equipped with requisite
Terrestrial tools
They simply walked
Because they could

Causing me to consider
The quandary of could and should
Before we met
I'd surf the old South Beach
Young Cubans boxers
Orthodox old men
Strolling by the sea
Seeking something
More aces than exile

By the time I brought you there
The ocean avenues cooked with
Cocaine vice and model chatter
The town seemed to sprint
On high stilettos

A kid grown up too quick
But if the shoe fits
Whose to know
When we're ready to run

I can only now say
(Three score and three years from the day)
We met in that bullseye high above middle path
I was too stunned
Too young
Undone by sea legs
I faltered on faults of my own
Unable to see
What you saw in me

People are the pools we step into
Limbs and lungs and loosening tails
Ready for the deep end
I shouldn't turn this into a story
(Like I always do)
Nor an apology (that too)
Just a world-stood-still
Gaze back wink
Here's looking at you

Mercury in Retrograde

Why are you sitting on the sidelines?

"When it's my will to say the whole is greater
I survey my parts, and wonder if I'm to be
The last living person to regard this line
Of thigh as no small matter

What vaunted few appreciate the tension
One hamstring engineers
Upon a multitude
To no subordinate end"

Get back in the game, Hermes
The world needs its messengers

No Exchanges Allowed

You'd cross the word *real* out
Any time I wrote it
Whatever it meant
To either then
We've travelled so far
From original intent
That our early avowals
Serve poor testament—
A divided skin grows too thin
We lack the miraculim
That tricks taste buds
To savor only sweetness
We can't decant
Early confidence
Hidden in plain sight
Fogged by hands breath
Searching the pane
Tracing the purpose
Remembered swoon
Proof enough

When one soul slips form
Enters another red sunset
Returns emerald flash
&
How softly and tenderly
Convergence vanishes
Only the colts of dream rear at
The gates of polished ivory
And translucent horn

Life is lived
Outside phantasm or truth
Dangling lines of slender silk
Beyond spring's specious argument

Rivers will recede
Other eyes will close
The lopsided moon will disappear
Erasure is

What is
real
            pockets filled with clementines
                              bus fare and matchless green

The Museums are Closed Today

Last night's dictionary
Of symbols failed
To contain the scene
You said
When my eyes were closed
    hello dream
When they opened
10,000 entries
Of me you imagined
And how did it feel
Finding my body useful
You who were there just trying to
Be romantic with low songs
Silver rider
Lady in gold
Steps off the wall to walk
At solstice through the park
Not to the conservatory
Nor the monkey bar
Things are swinging
At cafe des artistes
Said someone
Once hello
I knew
So well
Do you dream?

And We Shouted Verse to the Wind and Each Other

She stations us
Up to our knees in the mud
Of the shore throats fletched
To summon those who misbelieve

This is what we most need
To tilt our heads back
Receive the unexpected burst
From a thunder clap sky

Dizzy and fierce
Because indeed
The body knows
That it wants

Before it knows
What it wants
Galloping
In the saddle

Finger wed to string
We will send bird-throated
Arrows singing
To the furrowed flux

Scattering
Words in corduroy
Waves planting seeds
Making rain

Entrance

I must open the door!
This morning's glorious
Tangle of pantherine phrases
Needs a run and already
I stumble outpaced by this mad guileless
Inside tribe of cave-raised beasts
Straining at chains to pull melody
Free from all that
Spills up my sleeve
Like coffee spreading
Thoughts the way they do
When I'm trying to sleep
Always lying there
Arms stretched to be disarmed
By the action end
Of a long fingered lead — but not
I am tongue-tied
When you're not there
And I am tired of knots that won't open
So I shall call upon the felt self
Of smocked velvet and patterned tights
Of bare shoulders and cold feet
Of doves and groves and close confessions
We have loved too long
To puzzle along with
Winks and careless laughter
Here I am
Not "trying to say"
But saying
In my best shore-tested
Outside voice
Here I am
Open your door

Second Skin

like your mouth when you sleep
words present in absence
once
       minus
one
       one into *ocean*
one from the sum of *home* and *yonder*

one's intention is forever dividing
away from its lone integer
tailoring new endings
      (and cheers to that!)
we should give something up
for the brilliance of projections
like the ones that set night water to blaze
           with hidden fish
for clear is the screen
upon which we cleave
          conceit
extending metaphor
beyond even this most human act

i am lava   i am ice
    burning and breaking
    across continents
bouldering
       the frank
         ecology of intimacy
between each lifeline
traced from thumb to wrist
below the fleshy edge
where palm pounds fist
there lies an inner stamp
cleaving *end* from *need*
— and there
& then

we go down
we look down
we walk   we touch
   we talk
we speak up   we look
up   we look back

we see
polysemy
everywhere written
                    a multiverse

— for there it is
the meaning of all is
all meaning —

the word bridge to no man's land
where *one* parts from *alone*
— says floe flowing magnanimous magma
mouth that is not mine —

you have a body
you have a body
you have a body

Word Cave

I took you
From frost hollow
In the heat of my cheek
For the count of grace
Until movement returned
Gently releasing you
At the mouth
Of my private darkness go
Within you will find
Fire sticks that warm
Like my tongue
Flaring shapes
On the veined stone
Elongating our path
In brine from water to steppe
We have learned upright reckoning
We have arrived
By selvage and muscle spindle
To fashion the wind
As wand into word
Your lips into eyes
For the others
Speak

Credits

"These Ithakas" and "Impression of a Lone Arc Floating" first appeared as separate single-sheet broadsides (Oakland: Impart Ink Press, 2016) printed by Nicholas James Whittington at Dependable Letterpress;

"Imaginary Landscape" first appeared in Lightning Strikes: 18 poets. 18 artists. (San Francisco: Dolby Chadwick Gallery, 2015);

"Ode Abridged" first appeared in Everything Indicates: Bay Bridge Poems & Portraits (Berkeley: Heyday Books, 2012), eds. Ben Davis, Elissa Perry, and Tamsin Smith;

"Step" first appeared as a companion verse to the compressed documentation of Ana Teresa Fernandez' La Llorona performance in West Oakland, presented at Galeria de la Raza, San Francisco, 2011;

"Quatrefoil" first appeared in the program for the memorial for Dr. Allan D. Callow, Presidio Observatory, San Francisco, 2016;

"The Clue to an Idle Inheritance" and "S Curve" first appeared in the exhibition program Vacancies: New Works by Josh Smith (San Francisco: a.Muse Gallery, 2016);

"Vacancy" first appeared as a mixed media broadside at the Welcome to the Left Coast art exhibition presented by Luggage Store Cultural Center, San Francisco, 2016;

"Full Fathom Five" first appeared in Intimate Terrain: Series I and II (San Francisco: The McLoughlin Gallery, 2016);

"An Arc for the Frozen Sea" first appeared in the online publication Arc Fusion Magazine (San Francisco, 2016), to inaugurate an ongoing series featuring Tamsin Smith as poet in residence;

"The Collector" and "Cut-Up" first appeared in the exhibition program EMIC/ETIC: New Works by Vanessa Woods (San Francisco: a.Muse Gallery, 2016);

"Abacus of Right Action" first appeared in a broadside to accompany its inaugural reading at the Resnick Aspen Action Forum (Aspen, The Aspen Institute, 2016).

"Center Ring: Head v. Heart" "Lullaby" and "Eros Epicentered" first appeared Love in the Face of Everything (San Francisco: Mount Tamalpais Press, 2017).

"How is it that your live, and what is it you do?" first appeared in a broadside to accompany its inaugural reading at the Resnick Aspen Action Forum (Aspen, The Aspen Institute, 2017).

About the Author

Tamsin Spencer Smith is a poet and essayist. This is her first published collection and represents verse written since 2011, when she began crafting poems in earnest. She was born in Cambridge, England and moved to the United States at a young age with her father, a lepidopterist, and mother, a cell biologist. She graduated from Kenyon College with highest honors in English Literature, where she wrote her thesis on Vladimir Nabokov. She indulges by listening to all forms of music, including silence, plays with oil paints, surfs when she can, and is already at work on a new volume of poetry.

About the Artists

Front Cover Portrait of the Artist by Emilio Villalba, 2017 oil on wood. Villalba is San Francisco based artist and MFA graduate of the Academy of Art University. He is represented by Modern Eden Gallery. www.emiliovillalba.com/

Back Cover by San Francisco Artist Matt Gonzalez — detail of found paper collage 2016, from the collection of Charlie Pendergast and Kevin Connor. www.dolbychadwickgallery.com/artists/matt-gonzalez

Inside flap photographs by Bay Area photographer Josh Smith. www.joshsmithphoto.com

Inside cover photo of the poet on the beach, Key Biscayne, Florida, taken by Una Ryan, in the late 1970s. www.uluxart.com

All sales of this book will benefit Sites Unseen, a public art project designed to revitalize and activate underused San Francisco alleys with dynamic arts programing and happenings. www.sitesunseen.org/

Colophon

This book was set in
10 point Palatino Linotype
and printed in China by
Global PSD
www.globalpsd.com